Confidence

The Nice Guy Myth - How to Get What You Want in Love and Life without Being a Pushover

By

Stuart Killan

© **Copyright 2018 Stuart Killan - All rights reserved.**

The content contained within this book may not be reproduced, duplicated or transmitted without direct written permission from the author or the publisher.

Under no circumstances will any blame or legal responsibility be held against the publisher, or author, for any damages, reparation, or monetary loss due to the information contained within this book. Either directly or indirectly.

Legal Notice:

This book is copyright protected. This book is only for personal use. You cannot amend, distribute, sell, use, quote or paraphrase any part, or the content within this book, without the consent of the author or publisher.

Disclaimer Notice:

Please note the information contained within this document is for educational and entertainment purposes only. All effort has been executed to present accurate, up to date, and reliable, complete information. No warranties of any kind are declared or implied. Readers acknowledge that the author is not engaging in the rendering of legal, financial, medical or professional advice. The content within this book has been derived from various sources. Please consult a licensed professional before attempting any techniques outlined in this book.

By reading this document, the reader agrees that under no circumstances is the author responsible for any losses, direct or indirect, which are incurred as a result of the use of information contained within this document, including, but not limited to, — errors, omissions, or inaccuracies.

Table Of Contents

Your Free Gift

Introduction

Chapter One: What Makes You a Pushover

   Pleasing

   Neediness

   Exaggerating Compliments

   Defensive

   Lying

   Overworking

   Never Expressing Your Thoughts

   Uncertainty

   Apologetic

   Timid

Chapter Two: How to Give Compliments

Chapter Three: How to Respond to Backhanded Compliments

Responding to Backhanded Compliments
  Ignore it
  Thank them
  Only Acknowledge the Positive Portion
  Address the Insult
  Always Keep Your Sense of Humor

Chapter Four: Why should You Avoid Exaggerated Compliments

Chapter Five: Why Should You Laugh at Yourself

Chapter Six: How to Make Fun of Others without Hurting Them

  Teasing Your Friends

  Differentiate between Fun and Cruelty

  Make Fun of their Intelligence

  Use Metaphors and Similes

  React Dramatically

  Know When to Joke

  Know When to Stop

  Learn to Take it Well

Conclusion

Your Free Gift

As a way of saying thank you for downloading. I'm offering a free bonus report called *7 Habits of Highly Confident People* that's exclusive to the readers of this book.

Get instant access at http://freeconfidencebook.com

Inside the book you'll discover

- Secrets of The Joker, and why he should be admired
- The one thing confident people *always* do first when confronted with a tough situation – learning this alone can 10X your self esteem
- How to use vision boards to achieve your goals
- Identifying your "hidden talents" – even if you don't think you have any

- The one trait you must MURDER if you are to become successful
- How to never doubt your own abilities again
- Michael Jordan's #1 success secret
- The 4 most dangerous words in your vocabulary (if you're saying these regularly you are killing your own confidence)
- How to succeed as an introvert in an extrovert's world

Download for free at http://freeconfidencebook.com

Introduction

I want to thank you for purchasing the book, 'Shyness: The Nice Guy Myth - How to Get What You Want in Love and Life without Being a Pushover.'

People often believe that being nice is synonymous to being a pushover. It is because of this assumption that people who are nice are often advantage of. This may make you think twice about being nice to people. However, it does not have to be that way. You can be nice to people and still take a stand for yourself. If you want to learn how you can do this, you have come to the right place.

Over the course of the book, you will learn how you can be nice to people without being a pushover. You will learn about the things that you can do or say to avoid doing something that you do not want to.

I hope you gather all the information necessary.

Chapter One: What Makes You a Pushover

It is important to be nice if you want to be successful. This quality helps you maintain relationships since people will want to spend time with you; however, there is a thin line between being a pushover and being nice.

When you are too nice, you often make your way through life by placating the people around you. This makes it easy for people to push you over. You may want to take charge n many situations but are worried that you will come off as overbearing or having your opinion. This fear will make you submissive and give people the opportunity to extract work from you.

People who are pushovers often exhibit the characteristics listed below.

Pleasing

People often change their position or soften their opinion when they believe that the people around them will not receive their thoughts and opinions well. If you want to be successful, it is important that you communicate your thoughts and opinions. Instead of trying to please everybody, you should demand that they treat you with respect. If you try to please people in your workplace, you will realize that you are working on tasks that you do not want to do. You will find it difficult to tell people what you think about a specific task since they will not listen to what you have to say. Therefore, it is important that you educate yourself and become an expert in the field you are working in. This education will help you sound confident when you communicate your opinions.

Neediness

When you are too nice, you constantly seek approval from the people around you. It is important to remember that people cannot help you feel worthy. You cannot expect to succeed in life by coat-tailing another person. You can only succeed if you believe in yourself and are willing to stick to your beliefs regardless of what someone says to you. There are times when you need something from others. In those situations, ask yourself if you can get what you want without another's help. You must remember that what you want is important, and there are times when what you want will cause inconvenience to someone else. The only way you can get what you want is by saying what you want and going after it.

Exaggerating Compliments

It is hard to trust someone whose sentence begins and ends with a compliment. The same goes for you. Do not start and end a conversation with a compliment since that is manipulative. You only compliment these people since you are unable to handle your insecurities any other way. People often believe that they have secured another's approval if they feel good about it. You can only be successful when you are confident and not by pleasing another person.

Defensive

People will consider you weak when you are defensive. There are times when people will disagree with you. If you find it hard to deal with rejection, there is no path for you to succeed. You must develop resilience and accept criticism and feedback without being upset. People will not help you achieve success because they feel sorry for you. You must grow from constructive feedback.

Lying

When you have the innate need to please people, you become dishonest. You often agree with people when you do not believe in what they say. You should not be a parrot and accept or repeat everything they tell you. You will lose your identity. Your need to fit-in drives these actions. Successful people never try to fit in and are confident. They are strong to handle losses and are brutally honest whenever necessary.

Overworking

You overwork when you are desperate to prove your worth. When you have this attitude, you often work on tasks that you do not want to work on. When people sense that you are willing to do whatever it takes to prove your worth, they lose respect for you. You should learn to relax and do your part, and let others carry their weight.

You do not have to feel guilty about saying no,

and you do not have to participate in activities that you do not want to do. Your answer will define your likes and dislikes and make you a distinct individual. People will know where you wish to stop and they will pick up the tasks from there. If people do not know these boundaries, they will often push you to do more.

Never Expressing Your Thoughts

People will not value you when you fail to express your opinions and thoughts. There will be times when people will not listen to you since they believe you do not have an opinion. Ensure that you never withhold your values and opinions.

You must realize that conflict is a part of success, and learn to state your opinions without worrying about what people may say. If you are worried that someone may reject your opinion, one can never know what your preferences are or who you truly are. Never look for agreement, and always state what you believe is true.

Uncertainty

People pleasers often ask for permission in situations where they do not need to ask for permission. They do this because they want to look respectful and polite; however, you look unintelligent since they believe that you cannot make the simplest decisions.

You must be bold and lead the way regardless of whether you are uncertain. People fall in line when you are bold. The best way to overcome uncertainty is to believe in commit to what you believe in and work towards that belief.

Apologetic

When you start every sentence with the word 'sorry,' it gives people the idea that you have low self-esteem. You should never apologize for your existence. When you begin the word with 'Sorry, but,' you give people the impression that you expect them to disapprove your opinion. Always start the sentence with "Listen," since that will ensure that people pay attention to what you are saying.

Never worry about making mistakes. It is better to make mistakes than to disappear. When you change your answers to please another person, you are not being true to yourself. Remember that nobody is perfect and you do not have to apologize. Your mistakes are your greatest teachers. So, learn from them.

Timid

When you are timid, you let the fear drive you away from your passion and happiness.

Remember that you will never get anywhere by being timid and fearful. People are not sensitive and when you are timid. They will take advantage of you and will surpass you. You must find the confidence to pursue your passions. If you are timid, you follow your path aimlessly since you try to find a way to stay safe. Stay committed to your path.

The greatest irony is that when you are shy and timid, you allow people to do what they please with your life. To be successful, you must be confident about how you are or what you believe in. You must educate yourself and learn to be the best version of yourself. Keep learning until you reach the point where you have an opinion for yourself. You do not have to worry about whether you have the right opinion. Only when you embrace the differences, will you succeed. Remember that great ideas only come from debate. If you have some or all the qualities listed above, you should work towards changing how you think.

Chapter Two: How to Give Compliments

If you are shy, you will find it difficult to give compliments. People who are comfortable in situations always compliment the people around them. This chapter gives you some tips that will help you give good compliments and praise. It is important to learn this skill since it helps to start conversations and develop social bonds.

- Never give out compliments at random. If you do not believe in giving the compliment, you will come off as being insecure.

- Do not give a generic compliment. You should be specific about why you are giving them the compliment. For example, you can say, "Your eyes look beautiful" instead of saying "You look beautiful."

- Always consider the situation and the relationship you share with the person to ensure that the compliment is appropriate. If you want to give a comment that is personal, only give it to a friend in private.

- Always use creative words to compliment another. You can say, "Your dress looks beautiful and brings out the color of your eyes." Such compliments stick longer.

- Find opportunities to compliment a person's character and traits instead of the appearance since people do not listen to those compliments. For instance, you can compliment a teacher for his ability to motivate his students.

- Always give constructive criticism since a compliment always means more to the other person when he or she knows that you are being honest.

- Compliment people who are in authority.

People at a higher position do not receive too many compliments and you will be surprised at the response you receive. Some people will willingly accept your compliment and welcome the feedback.

- When you compliment someone with low self-esteem, you should avoid inflated praise. Try to compliment their behavior and not their traits. Research shows that people with low self-esteem worry about their future when someone compliments their behavior.

When you have mastered the art of giving compliments, you will find that you are better at accepting them too. You must remember that you should always have a positive experience when you either give or receive compliments.

Chapter Three: How to Respond to Backhanded Compliments

Most backhanded compliments are mean-spirited; however, sometimes you may give backhanded compliments out of ignorance. People often give backhanded compliments when they are afraid that people will not accept them. They believe that it is cool to give backhanded compliments. When they give backhanded compliments, they do not have to worry about giving their true emotions away. Therefore, it is important to learn how to give backhanded compliments and how to respond to them.

Responding to Backhanded Compliments

Ignore it

Ignoring a comment does not necessarily mean

that you allow someone to push you around. When you do not say anything, you do not give away your power. It only sends the message that you do not value the other person's opinion enough to defend yourself. You can also prevent an argument.

You should ignore people when you know they are saying something only to grab your attention. If someone says, "Thank you for the meal today. It is about time you cooked for me," do not react to it.

Thank them

You do not have to defend your choices to someone if they insult you, because your answer won't help the situation. Rather than arguing about why the compliment or comment hurt you, you can thank them and walk away. You should take this approach only when the other person is ignorant. For example, if your grandmother were to say, "It is better to work in a company than to work from home. I am glad that you no longer sit at home, but work in an actual office."

Only Acknowledge the Positive Portion

Criticism and feedback are essential to improve one's performance; however, it is counterproductive to sugar coat feedback with compliments. You must acknowledge only the positive portion of the compliment to show the person that you do not accept passive-aggressive comments. For example, your boss may say, "It was wonderful to see how well you worked today. It would have been great had you worked the same last week." All you need to do is thank the person for observing how well you worked today.

Address the Insult

Backhanded compliments have a negative effect

on relationships. Therefore, it is best to acknowledge the issue directly. Otherwise, the comments can become snarky, which will affect your relationship. If you do not want hurtful comments to come in the way of your relationship, you should speak up. If your friend says, "This dress looks wonderful on you. It hides your curves." Respond to your friend by telling him or her what part of that comment hurt you. If the compliment comes as a surprise to you, address it later.

Always Keep Your Sense of Humor

There are times when you should not take the comments some people make too seriously. These people may either not know how to deal with their emotions or want to hurt you. You can respond with a little humor. Do not be snobbish. For example, if a colleague says, "Congratulations on the work trip to Switzerland. Maybe now you will be happy about work." You can respond to that colleague by saying, "Haha, thank you, but it sounds like you are happy to see me leave."

Chapter Four: Why should You Avoid Exaggerated Compliments

People welcome compliments if they do not sound insincere. It feels great if someone recognizes you for the work that you do or who you are. Most people succeed when they receive compliments since they can warm their hearts, drive away fear and self-doubt and give us confidence; however, praise has negative effects too. Often, praise is verbal bribery, and a person offers it only when he or she knows it will work in his favor. In this chapter, you will learn why you must avoid giving exaggerated compliments.

If you are insecure and require confirmation from external sources to feel good, you are susceptible to insincere praise that has a price attached to it. People often prey on those with low self-esteem, and they are adept at detecting such people. They know what to say to build your confidence and use you for their own benefit. This does not mean that you should be suspicious of the people around you. But, there are times when it would be a good idea to consider whether someone is praising you for their benefit. If someone's compliments are exaggerated or overblown, they have an ulterior motive, and you should find a way to understand their true intentions.

Let us look at six reasons why flattery and praise may sometimes be schemes to use you.

- If people are insecure, they will compliment you in a way that helps them fit better into your social cycle. There are some people who agree to everything you say to win your favor. If you are someone who does this, you must stop immediately. As mentioned earlier, you should never agree with something anybody says to secure your relationship with them. You should stay true to your opinion.

- Some people butter you up before they bring you to the bargaining table. They do this to ensure that you will agree to their bargain. These people ensure that they praise you enough to make you feel special, regardless of how you see yourself. Eventually, you will be willing to compromise with them and will bend yourself to their will. This is because you believe you are in a mutually beneficial relationship.

- There are times when people may praise you to extract a specific favor from you. This is closely related to the point mentioned above. They praise you to increase the possibility that you will comply with their needs. They will gift you with praise and flattery, which will compel you to agree to their needs and desires. It is easy for them to take advantage of you to fulfill some deep desire. You may also lap up this praise since it fulfills your need to fit in. In such situations, you will find it difficult to differentiate between genuine and fake compliments.

- If you have fallen out with the person because of his or her behavior, they may resort to flatter to get back in your good books. If they can make you feel vindicated or supported, you will feel better about them. The probability that you will forgive them will increase when you fall for their insincere praises. You may then give the relationship a second chance or maybe a third.

- If people are unethical or shameless, they will offer you praise to ensure that you confide in them alone. You may also feel 'comfortable' about sharing some important information with them. Once they have this information, they will use it against you, either passively or aggressively depending on the situation.

They will take advantage of the position they are in by betraying your trust and pursuing their agenda. In the workplace, this can mean that the person will steal the promotion that you should receive. When you trust their praise, they have the chance to trick you into their confidence and exploit your trust in them.

- Another reason people compliment others is to manipulate them into behaving in a specific way. For example, in the Big Bang Theory, Sheldon gives Penny a treat every time she behaves 'well'. Most people give exaggerated compliments because they want you to comply with their whims and fancies. These praises will make you believe that you are good or worthy only when you behave the way people expect you to. This type of behavior leads to psychological abuse.

Chapter Five: Why Should You Laugh at Yourself

Research has shown that it is healthy to laugh at yourself. A study conducted by a team at the Mind, Brain and Behavior Research Center in Spain concluded that a person is happier when he or she makes self-deprecating jokes. This conclusion contradicts many other studies previously conducted on this topic since self-deprecating jokes were closely associated with poor mental health.

Jorge Torres Marin said that one could only make jokes about themselves if he or she is happy and social to an extent. The specifics of the findings are dependent on where you live. If people around you are comfortable with laughing at themselves, you may find it easier to laugh at yourself. Therefore, Marin wants to conduct more research on the topic to create a map of where one can feel free to laugh at themselves. He believes that culture plays an important role in this instance.

Marin mentioned that the phrase 'sense of humor' led to negative conclusions in previous studies. Many cultures define the phrase differently, which made it difficult for early research to understand why self-deprecating humor is good for you. There are two reasons why it was difficult to conclude this.

- Not everybody finds the same topics funny. If people are of different cultures, they will certainly find different subjects funny. For example, someone from England may not find baseball humor funny, but someone from the USA will find those jokes funny if he or she does not support the team.

- Another reason it was difficult to study humor was that people express it differently. Different behavior and a variety of comments can be humorous, and this variety overwhelmed researchers. This made it difficult to conclude why it is good for one to laugh at himself or herself.

However, Marin and his team did not create any boundaries while working on their hypothesis. Another researcher from the team, Hugo Dios, said that their research aimed to overcome every boundary. Marin and his team-studied behavior related to humor and classified that humor into adaptive and harmful humor. They broke different styles and types of humor down and explained that adaptive humor helped to strengthen relationships; however, self-enhancing humor only worked in stressful situations.

These styles of humor are closely related to a person's physiological wellbeing and can also be related to concepts like depression and anxiety. The team concluded that people who laugh at themselves know how to curb anger, but they cannot manage anger well. Therefore, it is acceptable to laugh at yourself occasionally. It shows people that you do not mind making fun of yourself.

Chapter Six: How to Make Fun of Others without Hurting Them

It is a good way to make friends by learning to tease people the right way; however, you should make sure that the other person shares the same sense of humor as you. You can also make fun of others if they are mean to you or to the people around you. Conversations flow with hilarity when you tease your friends.

Teasing Your Friends

When you tease your friends, you can be sarcastic. When you use sarcasm, you imply that your friend is being silly by asking you a reasonable question.

- You can twist your answer when someone asks you a question.
- Give your friends answers that are

obviously wrong.

- Try to exaggerate any response.

Differentiate between Fun and Cruelty

It is funnier and better to tease someone about something that is not the truth. If you have a friend who gets bad grades do not call him or her out in front of everybody else. He or she may be sensitive about it and it is cruel to draw attention to it. However, if your friend is a straight A's student, you can make fun of how bad he studies because that is the exact opposite of who he is.

Make Fun of their Intelligence

You can tease someone about how smart they are. If you know that the person does not mind if you make fun of their intelligence, go ahead and crack appropriate jokes. For example, you can say, "Please stop talking now. We are becoming wiser."

Use Metaphors and Similes

You can use some weird metaphors and similes to make fun of someone. These do not have to make sense, but people will laugh their heart out if the similes are weird. If someone is constantly annoying you, you can say, "You are like the Hulk of being extremely annoying."

React Dramatically

There are times when you do not have to say anything to make fun of your friend. You can react dramatically to something your friend said as if it is the silliest thing you have ever heard.

Exhale loudly, let your head fall backward, pretend you are asleep or roll your eyes.

Know When to Joke

It is important to learn when to crack a joke or make fun of someone. The timing can help someone differentiate between whether a person takes a joke in good faith. You must wait for the right opportunity to make a sarcastic comment. Pause after the joke to see how your friend received it. If he or she is upset, apologize to them immediately.

Know When to Stop

It is important to know when to stop. You cannot make fun of people or take it too far. Ensure that the person you are making fun of knows that you are joking. If you notice that they have taken the joke personally, stop. You should never hurt someone by picking on them. If someone is upset, apologize to them right away and let them know that you were only making fun of them.

Learn to Take it Well

If you make fun of people, they will make fun of you too. Learn to take it in the right stride. If you react negatively to every joke made about you, people will not speak to you or make fun of you.

Conclusion

Thank you once again for purchasing the book.

People believe that a person who is shy is a pushover and they take advantage of it. These people use that quality until it benefits them. If you are shy, you may have noticed that people make you do work that you do not want to do and do not listen to your opinions. It is time you change that.

Over the course of this book, you will learn how you can be a nice person without being a pushover. If you use the techniques mentioned in this book, you will never come across as a mean person.

I hope you have gathered all the information you are looking for.

www.ingramcontent.com/pod-product-compliance
Lightning Source LLC
Chambersburg PA
CBHW071039080526
44587CB00015B/2694